100 SCREEN-FREE WAYS o beat BOREDOM!

Quarto is the authority on a wide range of topics.
Quarto educates, entertains and enriches the lives of our readers—enthusiasts and lovers of hands-on living.
www.quartoknows.com

© 2018 Quarto Publishing plc

First published in 2018 by QED Publishing,
an imprint of The Quarto Group.
The Old Brewery, 6 Blundell Street,
London N7 9BH, United Kingdom.
T (0)20 7700 6700 F (0)20 7700 8066
www.QuartoKnows.com

ISBN: 978-1-78493-264-0

A catalogue record for this book is
available from the British Library.

Manufactured in Dongguan, China
TL062018

9 8 7 6 5 4 3 2

Editor: Emily Pither
Designer: Clare Barber

PICTURE CREDITS

Cover
Shutterstock: 279photo Studio, Africa Studio, akepong srichaichana, Aleksandr Simonov, AlexussK, Butsaya, honobono jack1986, M. Unal Ozmen, seeyou, sspopov, urbanbuzz

Interior
Shutterstock: 13Smile, 21, 279photo Studio, 17, A N D A, 75, 76, Aaron Amat, 1, 6, 54, Abel Tumik, 4, 5, 31, Abramova Elena, 54, 55, Africa Studio, 16, 24, 32, 43, 48, 54, 70, 74, Aigars Reinhold, 89, akepong srichaichana, 51, 55, 58, Aleksandr Simonov, 75, AlenKadr, 63, Alexander Gospodinov, 76, Alexandr Makarov, 63, AlexussK, 38, Alimag, 89, AlinaMD, amino, 22, 35, 43, 58, 10, 19, 38, 76, andersphoto, 58, Andrey Armyagov, 27, Andrey Burmakin, 25, Andrey_Kuzmin, 52, 80, 81, ANURAK PONGPATIMET, 21, Art Stocker, 58, 74, 86, artproem, 90, Asif Sattar, 53, Babich Alexander, 16, Bardocz Peter, 75, Beautyimage, Becky Starsmore, 9, 14, 15, bergamont, 37, 74, Bernd Schmidt, 22, 23, 29, 35, bestv, 74, Billion Photos, 37, bluesnote, 53, bonchan, 59, Brian A Jackson, 29, Butsaya, 11, 71, 75, Canadapanda, 42, CatherineL-Prod, 53, CHAIYARAT, 37, chen peng, 74, Chones, 60, clearviewstock, 46, Code2707, 93, colors, 29, 67, CWIS, 93, cynoclub, 50, Danny Smythe, 73, 93, De Visu, 9, 20, Designsstock, 93, Dewitt, 57, Dima Zel, 87, Dja65, 8, 15, Dmitrij Skorobogatov, 23, donatas1205, 25, Dora Zett, 37, Elena Shashkina, 17, Elnur, ericlefrancais, 35, ESB Professional, 51, escova, 61, EvgeniiAnd, 12, 13, 35, 59, Evgeny Karandaev, 23, exopixel, 44, ffolas, 1, 6, 54, Gabriele Maltinti, 88, Gargantiopa, 85, Goran Bogicevic, 10, gorra, 95, gowithstock, 46, Grand Warszawski, 83, GrashAlex, 27, Hedzun Vasyl, 22, Hhelene, 51, Hong Vo, 50, honobono, 38, hxdbzxy, 68, 69, levgenii Meyer, 69, ILYA AKINSHIN, 63, Imageman, 54, irin-k, 28, Isarapic, 77, 92, jack1986, 38, Jacqui Martin, 89, Jeanette Dietl, 61, Jenn Huls, 78, jesadaphorn, 94, Jules_Kitano, 93, K-Smile love, 58, Kaesler Media, 85, 87, 92, 95, Kard, 60, 75, kayralla, 15, Khumthong, 50, Konstantin Kopachinsky, 88, koosen, 24, Kotyk Inna, 8, 21, Kriengsuk Prasroetsung, 51, LDWYTN, 30, Levent Konuk, 42, Levgenii Meyer, 76, LilKar, 66, 67, 78, LittleMiss, 87, 92, 95, liza54500, 47, Logutenko, 81, Lotus_studio, 83, Lucie Lang, 81, Luis Carlos Torres, 21, Lukiyanova Natalia frenta, 78, Lunatictm, 45, 71, M. Unal Ozmen, 34, 35, Macondo, 54, Madlen, 52, MaleWitch, 30, margouillat photo, 76, marilyn barbone, 31, marla dawn studio, 17, Masterchief_Productions, 19, 63, Matteo Ceruti, 88, Mc Satori, 10, 78, 79, Michael Cyran, 41, 76, Militarist, 62, ml, 84, MNI, 60, Mr Doomits, 64, MSG64, 6, 26, Napat, 76, Narathaya Phankaew, 51, Nataliia Dubynska, 82, 19, Nataliia K, 65, natrot, 12, Nattika, 74, Nicescene, 60, NIPAPORN PANYACHAROEN, 74, Nuttapong, 71, oksama2010, 47, Oleg Lopatkin, 79, 94, Oleksandr Kovalchuk, 57, Oleksandr Lytvynenko, 55, 67, Oleksandr Rybitskiy, 54, Oliver Hoffmann, 69, Olyina, 80, OoddySmile Studio, 18, Pairaj Sroyngern, 43, 46, Palokha Tetiana, 19, Palto, 90, panuwat panyacharoen, 74, Paul Cowen, 46, PavelShynkarou, 41, Peter Gudella, 80, 94, 94, Peteri, 8, 9, 15, photka, 54, 55, 76, 93, 7, 33, 81, PI, 14, Picsfive, 57, pio3, 92, PLUKCHI ANATOLII, 30, primopiano, 4, 5, 8, 9, 20, 21, 34, 42, 54, 68, 78, Pushba, 86, rangizzz, 36, 70, Rashevskyi Viacheslav, 79, Rawpixel.com, 21, 78, Roman Samokhin, 40, 41, 79, Rosa Jay, 73, 77, Ruslan Semichev, 6, 26, 56, SchubPhoto, 45, SeDmi, 66, seeyou, 59, seramo, 89, serg78, showcake, 44, simpleman, 45, sspopov, 77, 96, Stockforlife, 45, Subbotina Anna, 8, 15, Svietlieisha Olena, 84, Sylvia Biskupek, 37, Tamisclao, 32, Tatiana Popova, 68, 69, taweesak thip rod, 41, Thitisan, 77, Thomas Soellner, 25, Tiger Images, 74, TrashTheLens, 40, Travel landscapes, 74, Triff, 75, 76, 78, Twin Design, 49, 61, 77, Ugorenkov Aleksandr, 89, urbanbuzz, 3, 91, Valentina Proskurina, 74, valkoinen, 10, 56, 65, Vangelis Vassalakis, 30, 37, Vastram, 50, VDP, 29, Viktor1, 18, Vitaly Korovin, 18, 51, Vladimir Sazonov, 79, Vladyslav Starozhylov, 49, 77, Volodymyr Krasyuk, 43, vvoe, 9, 14, 15, watin, 48, 61, 62, 70, WeStudio, 82, xpixel, 18, 50, Yellow Cat, 22, 67, 78, Yuri Samsonov, 46.

100 SCREEN-FREE WAYS

to beat BOREDOM!

Kris Hirschmann   illustrated by Elisa Paganelli

Contents

Beat Boredom on the Move

Hey Kids! Look Away from Your screen!

Texting, social media, apps, games, films, TV, streaming videos...

All of these digital delights are great ways to keep you entertained if you're bored, but there's a real world out there, too! It's an exciting world full of people, animals, food, games and fun!

This book is packed with 100 screen-free activities for you to try. There are loads of great things you can do AND plenty of cool ideas for your friends and family to join in with. Put that device down and get creative. Pick a page and try out something new!

Hey Grown-ups!

Want to Know More?

Tired of asking your child to put down their mobile phone?

Worried about how many hours your child spends watching TV?

Whilst much can be gained by using electronic devices, from learning to entertainment, excessive screen time has been linked to poor school performance, childhood obesity and attention problems.

The World Health Organisation has warned that a dramatic increase in screen time is putting children's health at risk. To help reduce this risk, It's important for parents and carers to take charge of setting limits on screen time.

Don't despair! Take a break from technology and provide your child with screen-free stimulation. This book contains a variety of activities and projects that can be completed easily and frequently, without requiring lots of expensive materials, equipment, or planning. The activities promote face-to-face interaction, family time and imaginative play, all of which are important, but are often overshadowed by using electronics.

Why not try one activity a day, or set challenges for how many activities your child can complete during the holidays. Whether at home, outdoors or even on the move, don't use technology to keep kids occupied while you focus on other things. Get active, get together and help your child beat boredom using screen-free ways.

BEAT Boredom at HOME

Bored of being stuck inside whilst it's raining? Grown-ups telling you to turn off the TV? Don't despair, try something else!

Here are 47 indoor activities for evenings, bad-weather days or anytime you just feel like staying at home. Featuring cooking, crafts, science and more, there's something for everyone.

Get off the sofa, invite your friends over and beat boredom together!

Pick-up Sticks

You don't have to buy an 'official' set to play this classic game of skill. You can improvise and make your own!

STEP 1

Assemble your set according to the table below. Any assortment of 'sticks' will do — pencils, skewers, craft sticks and so on. Just make sure the numbers match the table.

HELPFUL HINT
You'll need a collection of stick types and a specific number of each, as shown in the table below.

STEP 2

One player holds all of the sticks together vertically on a flat surface, then lets them go. The sticks will fall in a random pattern.

STEP 3

Players take turns trying to pick up one stick per turn. Only the stick the player is trying to take can move. If ANY other stick moves, the player loses that turn. If successful, the player gets to keep the stick.

Type	Number	Point value
1	1	25
2	7	10
3	7	5
4	7	2
5	8	1

STEP 4

When all of the sticks have been picked up, add up the scores. The player with the most points is the champion!

Try Some Yoga

Grab a mat or find a carpeted area and try some classic yoga poses.

DOWNWARD FACING DOG POSE

This popular pose stretches many muscle groups and lets blood flow to your brain, giving you extra energy. It also builds your strength.

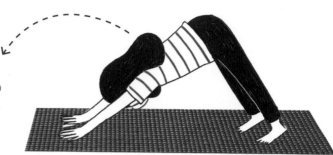

COBRA POSE

This pose stretches your spine and tummy and expands your chest, which is great for your heart!

TREE POSE

This pose is all about balance, posture and coordination. Stand steady, like a mighty tree!

CHILD POSE

This pose stretches your shoulders and back, and lets you relax fully. Close your eyes, shut out the world, breathe deeply and just chill!

Marshmallow Catapult

Why not ask your friends to build a quick and easy marshmallow catapult with you? It will provide hours of squishy, safe marshmallow-flinging fun! Whose marshmallow will fly the furthest?

STEP 4
Wrap a rubber band around the top of the cross shape to keep everything in place and to form the catapult shape.

STEP 1
Take five sticks and gather them into a neat pile. Wrap a rubber band around each end of the pile to hold the sticks together.

STEP 2
Place the pile sideways on top of another craft stick to form a cross shape.

STEP 5
To make the marshmallow holder, glue a plastic bottle top to the top of the upper craft stick.

STEP 3
Place another craft stick on top of the pile, lined up with the bottom stick. To secure, wrap two rubber bands around the centre of the cross shape where all of the sticks meet.

STEP 6
When the glue is dry, put a mini marshmallow in the bottle top. Set the catapult on a flat surface. Push down on the top craft stick, then release. Watch the marshmallow go flying!

12

Marshmallow Building

Take your imagination sky-high and start a marshmallow building project! Start with basic shapes and use mini marshmallows as connectors to join cocktail sticks into squares, triangles, pyramids and prisms.

Once you've mastered these simple shapes, join them to create bridges, buildings, or even towers — the bigger and more imaginative, the better!

Snowman Snacks

Reward yourself for your hard work with some tasty snowman snacks! Use a little bit of white icing to glue two large marshmallows together.

Add a red liquorice scarf to complete each snowman. These little chaps are ready to 'chill' out in your tummy!

Use coloured icing to add a face to the top marshmallow, and poke a pretzel stick through the bottom marshmallow for arms.

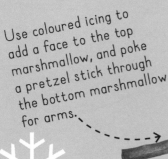

13

Painting with Acrylics

Painting is creative and fun, and acrylics are especially satisfying to work with. Grab some supplies and let your artistic side go wild!

WHY ACRYLIC PAINT IS GREAT

- It's non-toxic.
- It isn't smelly.
- It dries quickly.
- You can create different textures by spreading it thin or slapping it on thick.
- Because it's water-based, you can clean it up with water. No mess, no fuss!

WHAT YOU`LL NEED
- something to paint on – canvas, wood, paper, etc.
- acrylic paints
- brushes
- water
- paper plate (for paint mixing)
- paper towels

FUN IDEA 1
Mix sand, glitter or another substance into your paint to give it some extra personality.

T-shirt Friendship Bracelets

Do you have a drawer full of old, worn-out T-shirts? Try turning them into friendship bracelets for you and your friends. Wear them, share them!

WHAT YOU`LL NEED
- old T-shirts
- scissors
- loom bands or other small rubber bands

STEP 1
Ask an adult to help you cut a T-shirt into long, even strips that are about 2.5 centimetres wide.

FUN IDEA 2
Set up a still life (an assortment of objects). Try to paint it. How realistic can you be?

FUN IDEA 3
Try an abstract piece. Experiment with lines, patterns and colours. It's a masterpiece!

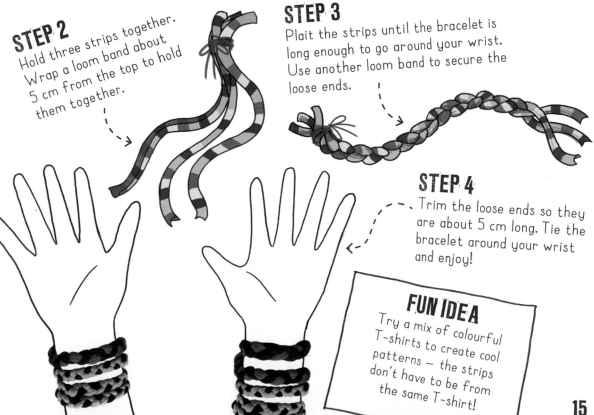

STEP 2
Hold three strips together. Wrap a loom band about 5 cm from the top to hold them together.

STEP 3
Plait the strips until the bracelet is long enough to go around your wrist. Use another loom band to secure the loose ends.

STEP 4
Trim the loose ends so they are about 5 cm long. Tie the bracelet around your wrist and enjoy!

FUN IDEA
Try a mix of colourful T-shirts to create cool patterns — the strips don't have to be from the same T-shirt!

15

Aluminium Alien Hats

HELLO, HELLO,

is there anybody out there?

If you turn your head into a big antenna, you might be able to pick up transmissions from aliens! Use aluminium foil to create the silliest hats you can imagine. Even if you don't make contact with any aliens, you'll have fun seeing who can invent the most outrageous headwear!

TIP

It might help to use a bicycle helmet or a silver colander as a base for your hat.

Cardboard Construction

Old cardboard boxes don't need to be rubbish!

Gather as many boxes as possible, ideally in a range of different sizes and use them like blocks to build big structures. Use packing tape to join them if you want your structure to be extra sturdy.

IDEAS FOR THINGS TO MAKE:
- castle
- cave
- bus
- house

banana brown owl

cucumber cat

Create an Artful Sandwich

Don't have the same boring old sandwiches for lunch every day. Turn them into art by adding sliced vegetables, cheese, olives, fruit and spread (but maybe not everything on the same sandwich!). The possibilities are endless! Here are a few ideas to get you started.

strawberry fish

peanut butter reindeer

Make Your Own Fingerprint Kit

Put your sleuthing skills to the test with this DIY detective fingerprint kit!

WHAT YOU'LL NEED
- two empty spice jars
- cornflour
- cocoa powder
- dry paintbrush or make-up brush
- sticky tape
- coloured paper
- washable ink pad

STEP 1
Put some cornflour in one jar and cocoa powder in another.

STEP 2
Find a hard surface you think might have a fingerprint hidden on it, such as a door handle or a mug.

STEP 3
If the surface is a light colour, sprinkle some cocoa powder and gently dust it with your brush. On a dark surface, use cornflour.

STEP 4
If you find a fingerprint, stick a piece of tape over it and then gently lift the tape off.

Is it a match?
Once you've collected your fingerprints, you'll need to match them to any 'suspects'. Ask your friends and family to press their fingertips onto a washable ink pad and then leave their fingerprints on a sheet of paper. Label the paper with each person's name. You now have a fingerprint database to match any you find with your kit!

ASK AN ADULT
Always check with a grown-up before you start sprinkling powder or cornflour.

STEP 5
Stick the tape onto a sheet of coloured paper, so you can see the fingerprint. Check it carefully against any fingerprints in your database. Can you tell who it belongs to?

Tornado in a Bottle

Pretend to be a scientist and make a tornado that you can hold in your hand!

WHAT YOU'LL NEED

- two empty clear, plastic 500 ml water bottles
- one water bottle top
- water
- food colouring
- glitter
- packing tape

STEP 1

Get an adult to help you poke a hole in the water bottle top. The hole should be about 1 centimetre wide.

STEP 2

Fill one bottle with water. Add a few drops of food colouring and some glitter, then screw the top on the bottle.

STEP 3

Place the second bottle on top of the first one. Tape the tops of the bottles together with packing tape to form an hourglass shape.

STEP 4

Hold your creation over the sink in case it leaks. Flip it over so the full bottle is on top. Swirl it in a steady circular motion a few times, then watch the water form a glittering tornado as it drains into the bottom bottle!

Origami Puppies

Even if you don't have a real puppy to play with, you can easily make an origami version instead! Woof, woof! You could even make a whole litter of puppies to keep your first dog company.

WHAT YOU`LL NEED
- sheets of square paper, any size
- black marker pen

HINT
You can use actual origami paper for this activity if you have it. If not, you can cut squares from normal paper.

STEP 1
Sit at a table and place the paper in front of you. Make sure it looks like a diamond with a point at the top rather than a square. Fold the top half of the paper down over the bottom half to make a triangle.

Museum of Me!

It's time to dig out any of your childhood photos and artwork and put them on display! Here are some ideas that will help you create your very own 'Museum of Me'.

Prepare
Go through your old photos, paintings, drawings, sculptures, collages and anything else you can find. Pick out the most impressive or meaningful pieces and display them in your room of choice.

Decorate
Make frames for your favourite pieces. You can cut strips of mount board, decorate them to look like fancy frames and tape them around the edges of your artwork.

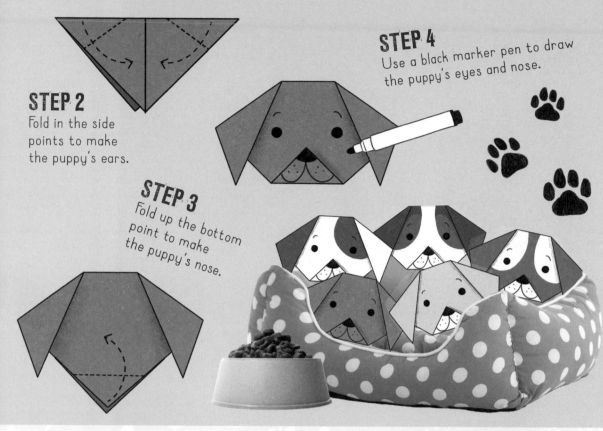

STEP 2
Fold in the side points to make the puppy's ears.

STEP 3
Fold up the bottom point to make the puppy's nose.

STEP 4
Use a black marker pen to draw the puppy's eyes and nose.

Share
Make invitations for your 'art opening'. Give them to your family and friends and wait for the crowds to arrive!

Explain
Create a small plaque for each piece of artwork, just like they do in real museums. Try to include the piece's title, the date it was created and a brief explanation.

Silly Slime

It's slime time! Did you know that slime is easy to make using just a few things from the kitchen? Here are two versions you can try. Why not invite your friends over and make both!

Wearing gloves, put the water and the food colouring into a bowl. Stir to mix. Add the cornflour little by little, continuing to stir. Your slime is done when you can stir it very slowly, but not quickly — it'll harden up and become solid if you do!

COLOURFUL SLIME
WHAT YOU`LL NEED
- rubber gloves
- 120 ml water
- food colouring (green works very well, but you can choose any colour you like!)
- 120 g cornflour

HINT
You may need to tweak the ingredients. If the slime is too thin, add a little cornflour. If it's too thick, add a little water.

SOAPY SLIME
WHAT YOU`LL NEED
- rubber gloves
- 60 ml liquid washing detergent
- 15 ml PVA glue

Wearing gloves, combine the washing detergent and glue in a bowl. Stir vigorously until the mixture thickens into a blob of slime. If necessary, tweak the ingredients to create the perfect consistency.

Write a Letter

They say letter writing is a lost art, but it doesn't have to be! Grab your pencils, pens and paper and write a real letter to a friend or relative.

For visual impact, decorate your letter with doodles, stickers or anything else that strikes your fancy. Stick the finished letter in an envelope, address it and add a stamp. Then drop it into a postbox and send it on its way. It's not as fast as e-mail, but it's much more special...and lots of fun, too!

Shaving Foam Sculpture

Use shaving foam (and your imagination!) to create your own sculpture!

STEP 1
Grab a can of cheap shaving foam (available at any pound shop).

STEP 2
Squirt a big mound into a dry sink or bath, or onto a wipe-clean surface, and see what you can do with it.

STEP 3
Try using spoons and craft sticks to shape the shaving foam. What will you make?

23

Paper Plate Snowflakes

You don't have to wait for winter to see snow! These easy paper plate snowflakes can be made any time of the year.

STEP 1
Fold the paper plate in half.

STEP 2
Fold back the side points evenly along the dotted lines, as shown in the illustration. The plate should now be a cone shape.

STEP 3
Use scissors to make your snowflake pattern by cutting away parts of the cone. Be creative!

Lip-sync Battle

A lip-sync battle takes karaoke to the next level of fun! Taking turns, each player picks and puts on his or her favourite song.

Without singing a note, each player must mime the words to the song as well as act it out with as much feeling and drama as possible. When everyone has taken a turn, vote to determine the winner. Who will triumph in the lip-sync battle? It's up to you!

STEP 4

Unfold the cone to see your finished six-sided snowflake. Tie a piece of string to it and hang your creation anywhere you like.

There's no reason to stop with one snowflake. Make a whole snowstorm and hang them around your home.

Talent Show

Everyone has some kind of talent! Gather some friends and put your skills on display in a talent show!

Set up a stage area and take turns performing. Make sure someone records the fun so you can watch your own performance later — and marvel at your friends' amazing abilities, too!

25

Volleyballoon

Organise a game of indoor volleyballoon that is safe for your furniture and windows as well as super fun!

WHAT YOU'LL NEED
- string
- large balloon
- a few teammates

STEP 1
Choose a room to be your volleyballoon court and move any furniture out of the way.

STEP 2
Stretch a piece of string across the room at head height, or a little lower. To secure, tie or tape the ends of the string to something at each end of the room. If this doesn't work, you can lay the string across the floor to split the room in half.

STEP 3
Divide your friends into two teams, one on each side of the string.

STEP 4
One team serves by hitting the balloon over the string. The other team tries to hit the balloon back. The game continues back and forth until the balloon touches the floor.

SCORING
When the balloon touches the floor, the opposite team gets a point and they get to serve. The first team to reach 10 points wins!

Domino Toppling

THE TURN
Arrange the dominoes so they fall in a u-turn and then head in the opposite direction.

THE STRAIGHT LINE
Practise spacing your dominoes evenly and precisely.

Line up some dominoes, knock the first one over and watch the whole row tumble! Can you master these patterns?

HINTS
Work on a flat, smooth surface.

Whilst you work, remove dominoes from the line every now and then to leave gaps. Then, if the line is knocked down by accident, it will stop before your hard work is ruined!

THE DIAMOND
The dominoes start from a single point, widen in opposite directions, then come back together to form a diamond shape.

THE SPLIT
One line of dominoes splits into two.

27

Charades

Charades has been a popular guessing game for hundreds of years and that's no surprise — it's a blast!

To play, each person in a group writes the titles of several films, TV shows or books on separate pieces of paper. All of the pieces then go into a bag.

Each player gets a turn pulling out a piece of paper, then acting out the title. The other players try to guess what it is. This is a game where success is satisfying, but mistakes are hilarious. Get ready to giggle!

Picture Perfect

This game is similar to charades, but it involves drawing instead of acting.

First, everyone needs to write a word (ideally a noun) on a piece of paper. Then take turns choosing a paper and drawing the chosen item whilst the other players try to guess the word. Good art skills are definitely helpful in this game, but anyone can succeed. Just draw FAST and think creatively. You may be surprised by your own artistic genius!

Homemade Modelling Dough

It's fun to sculpt with modelling dough, but what if you can't get to the shop to buy the 'proper' stuff? No problem. Make your own with this easy recipe!

HERE WE DOUGH!

Put the water, 15 ml of oil and the food colouring into a bowl. Stir to mix. Add the flour and salt, and squeeze with your hands to mix everything together. If the mixture seems too dry, add a little more oil.

HINT

Make several batches of dough in different colours so you can make multicoloured sculptures.

HINT

Store your dough in resealable plastic bags when you have finished sculpting. This will keep it from drying out.

Fashion Show

Have you ever dreamed about strutting your stuff on a high-fashion runway? Well, dream no more — it's time to do it! Here are some suggestions for staging your own event.

STEP 1

Every fashion show needs a theme. Do you want to display evening wear? Casual clothing? Accessories? Is your collection for spring/summer or autumn/winter? You're the designer, so you get to choose your approach.

STEP 2

'Hire' your models. You can tell them what to wear, or you can explain your theme and let them pick their own outfits, make-up, hairstyles and so on. Each model should have several 'looks'.

STEP 3

Clear space for your runway! Using two rows of chairs, create a long, narrow area for your models to walk down. The chairs will also be useful for your guests to sit and watch!

STEP 4

Invite an audience to your show. Put on some music, then let your models take turns on the runway for some fashion-forward fun!

Clothes Peg Butterflies

Let your creativity take flight with this easy and cute craft. Make as many adorable butterflies as you like!

WHAT YOU'LL NEED (FOR EACH BUTTERFLY)
- two cupcake cases
- wooden clothes peg
- PVA glue
- two googly eyes
- one 5 cm piece of pipe cleaner, bent in a V-shape

STEP 1
Fold the cupcake cases in half, then in half again, to make triangles.

STEP 2
Use the clothes peg to pinch the cake case triangles together so they are arranged like wings.

STEP 3
Glue on the googly eyes and pipe cleaner. Ta-da! Your butterfly is ready to take flight!

FUN IDEA
If you're using plain coloured cake cases, you can decorate them before folding them. Be creative and colourful!

Do-It-Yourself Balance Beam

HINT
A real balance beam measures about 10 cm wide by 5 metres long.

How's your balance? Could you be a top gymnast? Let's find out!

Use masking tape to make the shape of a balance beam on your floor. Try walking, hopping or even somersaulting on it. If you put a hand or a foot off to either side, oops! Game over!

Blow Track

Here's another great activity that only requires masking tape, a straw and a small ball.

Use masking tape to create a zigzag track over the floor. Make it as simple or as complicated as you like. Then, get down on your hands and knees and blow into the straw to direct the ball from the start of the track to the end. Try to keep the ball on the tape, because if it rolls off the track, you have to start again!

HINT
Depending on how wide your tape is, it might work best to use two strips of tape and then direct the ball between the lines.

Hoop Plane

This glider plane is super simple to make and is gentle enough to throw indoors. Try it and see!

WHAT YOU'LL NEED
- sheet of card
- scissors
- tape
- straw

STEP 1

From the sheet of card, cut one strip measuring 2.5 x 13 cm and one strip measuring 2.5 x 26 cm.

STEP 2

Bend the larger strip into a circle and tape the ends together to form a hoop.

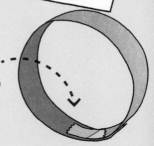

STEP 3

Repeat step 2 using the smaller strip.

STEP 4

Tape one circle to each end of the straw.

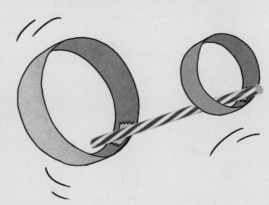

STEP 5

Hold the plane with the small hoop in front. Throw it, then watch it glide!

Ice Cream in a Bag

Why go to the shop when you can make ice cream at home? You don't even need a machine to do it — you only need a bag and a few simple ingredients!

STEP 1

Put the milk, sugar and vanilla extract into the small pastic bag. Seal the bag.

WHAT YOU`LL NEED

- 120 ml full fat or semi skimmed milk
- 1 tablespoon sugar
- ¼ teaspoon vanilla extract
- 1 small sealable plastic bag
- 1 big sealable plastic bag
- about 4 handfuls of ice cubes
- 150 g salt
- oven gloves

STEP 2

Put the ice cubes and salt into the big sealable bag. Then put the small bag in as well. Seal the big bag.

STEP 3

Put on oven gloves so your hands don't get too cold. Then squeeze and shake the big bag. After five to ten minutes, the ingredients in the small bag will freeze into delicious ice cream.

STEP 4

Remove the small bag, open it and dig right in!

FUN IDEA

Why not try your ice cream in a cone? Add all your favourite toppings!

Cocoa on a Stick

Cocoa on a stick? Good news! This snack is both delicious and easy to make.

INGREDIENTS
- 226 g chocolate chips
- 64 g icing sugar
- 28 g unsweetened cocoa powder
- marshmallows

EQUIPMENT
- microwave-safe bowl
- stirring spoon
- short wooden skewers
- ice cube tray

STEP 1
Put the chocolate chips into a microwave-safe bowl. Ask an adult to microwave them, heating for 30 seconds at a time and stirring between each cycle until the chocolate is completely melted.

STEP 2
Stir the icing sugar and cocoa powder into the chocolate to make a crumbly mixture. Spoon this mixture into an ice cube tray, making sure each section is full.

STEP 3
Poke a skewer into each section of the ice cube tray. Slide a marshmallow onto each skewer on top of the cocoa mix, then put the whole thing into the fridge to cool. When the chocolate is firm, it's ready to eat. DELICIOUS!

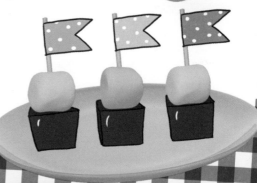

One-Minute Challenge

These challenges might sound easy, but they can be tricky if you only have a minute to complete them! Invite your friends over for a fun competition — who will be the fastest?

tick
tick
tick

WHAT YOU'LL NEED
- stopwatch or timer
- supplies for your games (this will vary depending on what you pick)
- paper and pencils to keep score

Put on a Play

It's theatre time! Together with your friends, come up with an original storyline for a play.

Think about the characters you'd like to see and choose performers for the different roles.

Assemble costumes, props and makeshift scenery, then go for it!

Don't forget to invite an audience — you'll want to hear them applaud after all your hard work!

CHALLENGES

1. Move a biscuit from your forehead into your mouth using your face — no hands allowed!
2. Balance an egg on its end.
3. Hang a spoon from your nose.
4. Keep three balloons off the ground at the same time by tapping them.
5. Blow a bubble through a hula hoop from a distance.
6. Stack twelve dice in a tower.
7. Flip five half-filled water bottles (with the tops on!) so they land upright.
8. Throw up and then catch ten bits of popcorn in your mouth.
9. Transfer ten small sweets from one bowl to another, using only a straw and your sucking power.
10. Knock over ten objects by swinging a yo-yo on its string.

Paper Bag Skits

For a totally off the cuff, theatrical experience, try some silly paper bag skits.

In this activity, each person gets a paper bag that contains five random items, chosen by a friend — the actor must not have any clue what's inside! The actors take turns opening their bags, removing the items and inventing a skit that includes them. Yes, ALL of them. Who will do the best job? There's only one way to find out!

Pet Stones

They're cute, they don't eat much and since they don't need walking, pet stones make perfect companions!

WHAT YOU'LL NEED
- a stone (ideally about the size of your palm)
- googly eyes
- glue
- permanent marker pens
- paints and paintbrushes
- a small box
- shredded paper

STEP 1
Take a quick trip outdoors to find a stone. Bring it inside and wash it well, then let it dry completely.

STEP 2
Glue googly eyes to your stone. Use permanent markers or paint to add other features, such as a mouth, nose, whiskers, ears, etc.

STEP 3
Decorate a small box to be your pet stone's bed. Don't forget to write your pet's name on it!

STEP 4
Shred some paper and put it into the decorated box to make a nest for your pet stone. Then place your pet in its new bed. So comfy and cute!

Stony McStoneface

Funny Photo Booth

They say a picture is worth a thousand words, but some photos are so hilarious, they might be worth even more! Set up your own funny photo booth and capture some one-of-a-kind images with your friends.

STEP 1

Collect or make a range of fun dress-up accessories. Hats, scarves, feather boas, hair accessories, sunglasses — anything you can wear or hold is fair game!

WHAT YOU'LL NEED

- dress-up items and silly accessories
- a solid-colour backdrop (e.g., a plain wall or a sheet)
- a camera, or a phone with a camera

STEP 2

Choose a combination of accessories to create your unique look. The sillier, the better!

STEP 3

Stand in front of your backdrop, either on your own or with a group. Get one friend or a parent to be the photographer. Strike a pose and snap, snap, snap away!

FUN IDEA

Cut out the centre of a large piece of dark-coloured stiff card, leaving a frame shape. Hold the frame up so you are peeking through it. Picture perfect!

Bubble Wrap Walkway

Pop, pop, POP! Make some joyful noise with a bubble wrap walkway that is easy to make and super fun to use.

Lay a long strip of bubble wrap down a hallway and use masking tape to hold the edges in place. Then walk, jump, roll, or dance up and down the hallway. Challenge your friends to walk across without popping any bubbles, or try popping EVERY bubble!

Indoor Snowball Fight

Even if it isn't snowing outside, make these fun, soft 'snowballs' and fire away!

WHAT YOU'LL NEED
- two sheets of scrap paper (per snowball)
- plastic wrap

STEP 1
Loosely crumple the sheets of scrap paper into a rough ball shape.

Indoor Bowling

A long hallway makes a perfect bowling alley. The walls act as built-in bumpers, so you'll never roll a ball into the gutter!

You'll need ten empty plastic water bottles and a big rubber ball. Set up the bottles in a tenpin bowling pattern, then take turns with your friends rolling the ball down the hallway and trying to knock the bottles down. Each player gets two goes to knock over all ten bottles. After two goes, the bottles are set back up for the next player's turn.

FUN IDEA

Use paper, tape and markers to decorate the water bottles like real bowling pins.

STEP 2

Pull off about a 46 cm sheet of plastic wrap and lay it on a table. Set the ball of paper at one end of the plastic wrap.

STEP 3

Roll the ball forwards, folding the plastic wrap inwards and smoothing it as you go. This will create an 'icy' coating around your ball.

STEP 4

Repeat steps 1 to 3 to make a pile of snowballs. Gather your friends and prepare for battle!

Painted Toast

Turn a simple slice of toast into a masterpiece by painting it with this quick and simple 'milk paint'.

FUN IDEA
Why not make painted toast as a special breakfast surprise for a family member's birthday, or for Mother's or Father's Day?

STEP 1
Set out a mug or bowl for each colour you want to use. Pour a little milk into each (about 1/4 mug).

STEP 2
Add a few drops of food colouring to each mug, until you are happy with the colour. Stir the milk paint to get an even colour.

STEP 3
Using a clean paintbrush, paint your picture onto a slice of white bread.

STEP 4
Toast your bread in a toaster on low heat.

STEP 5
Spread some butter on your toast and eat up!

TIP
Try not to put too much paint on the bread, or it will be soggy!

VEGAN OPTION
If you don't want to use milk, replace it with water.

Homemade Butter

Why not try making your own butter to spread on your toast? It tastes better when you use butter that you've made yourself!

STEP 1
Pour double cream into your jar until it's half full. Add a small pinch of salt, only if you like salted butter.

STEP 2
Tightly screw on the lid.

STEP 3
Now shake, *shake,* *shake,* This part will take a while — between 10 and 30 minutes — so be patient. You'll see a lump forming and growing inside the jar as you work.

STEP 4
When a solid, yellow lump has formed, pour out the remaining liquid.

STEP 5
Remove your lump of butter from the jar and let it dry on a paper towel.

STEP 6
Spread your homemade butter on a piece of bread! Delicious!

TIP
Your butter will last for a few days if you keep it in the fridge between uses.

43

Homemade Stress Ball

Stress balls feel great to hold and they're fun to squeeze. Follow these easy instructions to make your own.

STEP 1
Blow up the balloon to stretch it out. Let it deflate.

STEP 2
Insert the funnel into the balloon's neck. Carefully pour flour through the funnel until the balloon is full. Get as much flour in there as possible!

STEP 3
Tie off the balloon's neck, making the knot as close to the flour as possible. You want the ball to be nice and tight.

STEP 4
Squeeze and squash your homemade stress ball!

FUN IDEA
Use permanent marker pens to draw patterns or silly faces on your stress ball. Make it personal!

Line Dancing

A line dance is a choreographed routine, where many people do the same set of moves along with a song. Pick a favourite song and create your own line dance! You can use line dances you already know, or make up a totally original routine. It's up to you!

A FEW POPULAR LINE DANCES
- The Macarena
- The Electric Slide
- The Cupid Shuffle

Window Doodling

Your bedroom window is a perfect canvas for some decorating fun!

Clean the glass thoroughly to create a fresh surface. Dry it with a paper towel, then grab a pack of dry-erase markers and doodle away! You could draw spaceships, animals, random designs, or anything else you like. When you get tired of your designs, you can just wipe them off with a sponge or cloth and start all over again. Change things up every day, if you like — the choice is yours!

TIP
Always check with an adult first, and only use dry-erase markers for this activity as they are safe to use and can easily be wiped away. If you need help to wipe away your designs, try using a little water.

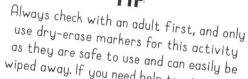

45

Biscuit Draughts

Are you in the mood for a game or a snack? You're in luck — this activity involves both!

WHAT YOU`LL NEED
- 30 x 30 cm sheet of white card
- ruler
- black marker pen
- one packet of brown biscuits
- one packet of white biscuits

STEP 1
Using a ruler, divide the card evenly into an 8 x 8 grid. Colour in alternating squares to make a black-and-white draughtboard pattern.

Indoor Picnic

Is it too rainy or cold outside to have a real picnic? That's no problem — you can have an indoor picnic instead!

STEP 1
Plan, make and pack a picnic lunch with your picnic pals. Remember, there's no kitchen or fridge on a real picnic. Make sure you do EVERYTHING in advance!

STEP 2
With a grown-up's permission, pick a room and move furniture out of the way to make your picnic area. Spread blankets on the floor and arrange a pile of comfy pillows and cushions.

STEP 2

Each player puts 12 biscuits on the black squares, as shown. One player has the brown biscuits on one side of the board, and the other player has the white biscuits on the other side of the board.

STEP 3

Now play the world's most delicious game of draughts. Yum!

THE RULES

- The goal is to take all of your opponent's biscuits.
- Each biscuit can only move forwards and diagonally one space per turn.
- A biscuit can jump over the opponent's biscuit if there is an empty spot on the other side. A player captures an opponent's biscuit by jumping over it.
- If a biscuit reaches the other side of the board, it gets a second biscuit stacked on top. Now it is a king and can move backwards as well as forwards.

STEP 3

Set the mood and put on some summery music.

STEP 4

Why not play some games at your picnic? Pull out some board games and have a tournament. You can have fun and eat tasty snacks at the same time!

BEAT Boredom
OUTDOORS

Leave your laptop or tablet at home and head outside for some fresh air.

Here are 26 activities to get you out of the house. Try some gardening, feed some birds, find some treasure and play all sorts of sports in your garden or a convenient outside space.

It's time to get moving and have some fun in the sun!

Easy Bird Feeder

Give your local birds a treat with this easy-to-make bird feeder.

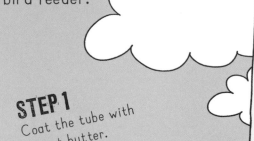

STEP 1
Coat the tube with peanut butter.

STEP 2
Roll the tube in bird seed. The seeds will stick to the peanut butter.

STEP 3
Slip a ribbon or string through the tube and tie the loose ends together in a knot.

STEP 4
Hang your bird feeder outside, then wait and watch. Soon your feathered friends will arrive for the feast!

Build a Bee House

WHAT YOU'LL NEED
- plant pot
- small lump of modelling clay
- straws

Bees are good for your garden. Encourage them to hang around by making a simple bee house!

Press the clay into the bottom of the pot. Push a handful of straws into the clay. Lay the pot sideways in a shady area and wait for the bees to move in. Bzzz, bzzz!

Close-up View

Your garden is crawling with life. Grab a simple magnifying glass, head outside and get a close-up view!

Just lie on the ground, lean down close, part the blades of grass with your hands and look through the magnifying glass. Give your eyes a moment to adjust. Before long you'll see all sorts of movement as tiny creatures shuttle back and forth before your eyes. There's no telling what you might see!

51

Map Quest

Ahoy, mateys! Pick a spot, hide some treasure, then make a map so your friends can search for it.

STEP 1
With an adult's help, bury your 'treasure' somewhere outside. Make sure it is hidden and protected (e.g., in a box).

STEP 2
Create a treasure map to show where the treasure is. 'X' marks the spot, of course! Include lots of landmarks.

STEP 3
Give the treasure map to your friends and let the quest begin! How long will it take them to find the buried treasure?

FUN IDEA
Include one small treasure (e.g., a sweet) for each treasure hunter. Don't forget to put in one for yourself, too!

Sky-Gaze in Style

instead of staring at your screen, turn your eyes to the sky! In the daytime, you might see clouds, birds, aeroplanes, butterflies and much more. But at night, you can marvel at the stars and Moon.

To sky-gaze in style, fill a dry paddling pool with pillows and blankets to make a cozy nest in your garden. It's not just comfy, it's insect-free, too!

Glow-in-the-Dark Ring Throw

Some inexpensive glow sticks and necklaces from the pound shop make a great glow-in-the-dark ring throwing game.

Push glow sticks into the ground and use necklaces as rings. Set up a 'course' all over your garden and play the night away. GLOW for it!

Herb Garden

Growing herbs is fun, easy AND tasty!
Here's how to start your own herb garden.

WHAT YOU'LL NEED
- gardening gloves
- herb seeds
- small pots, or a spot in your garden
- soil
- water

STEP 1

Put on some gloves and follow the directions on the seed packets to plant your herbs. You can plant the seeds in pots using some soil, or plant them straight into the ground in your garden — it's up to you!

Build an Obstacle Course

You don't need special equipment to build your own obstacle course.

All you need is a bit of imagination, some household objects and the willingness to get off the sofa! If you don't have a garden, you can still make a course in your local park. Just make sure your 'obstacles' are portable and bring some friends along to help you.

Arrange old bricks on the ground to use as stepping stones.

STEP 2

Make sure your pots have enough sunlight to help the seeds grow and water your pots daily. Weed the area if you have planted your herbs in the ground. Soon you should see small sprouts.

STEP 3

When your herbs grow big enough, carefully pull or cut off leaves and shoots to season your food. Delicious!

FUN IDEA

Why not choose a theme for your herb garden?
- Pizza herbs: basil, parsley, oregano
- Salsa herbs: coriander, parsley
- Sandwich herbs: chives, dill
- Tea herbs: chamomile, mint

Use old cuddly toys or empty cardboard boxes as hurdles to jump over.

Fill up water balloons to throw at a target.

Open up the ends of an old cardboard box to crawl through like a tunnel. Tape boxes together to make a longer tunnel.

Water Balloon Piñatas

When it's really hot outside, this game will keep you cool!

STEP 1
Ask an adult to tie a thick rope between two trees outside, about 2 metres above the ground.

STEP 2
Fill several balloons with water until they are nice and plump. Tie them shut, then tie them to the rope (you can just knot the balloons' necks around it). Leave a gap between each balloon.

STEP 3
Blindfold a friend and guide them to the balloons. Give them a bat, stand back and let the swinging begin! How many balloons will burst after three swings?

STEP 4
Replace any burst balloons, then let the next person have a turn. Continue until all the balloons are burst or everyone is soaking wet, whichever comes first!

Slip and Slide!

Slip and slide the hot summer days away with this fun and easy activity.

WHAT YOU`LL NEED
- a large plastic tarpaulin — the bigger, the better
- washing-up liquid
- a hose with a spray nozzle

STEP 1
Spread some tarpaulin on the ground.

STEP 2
Drizzle a small amount of washing-up liquid onto it. Try and spread the liquid evenly to get drops onto every part of the tarpaulin.

STEP 3
Spray a little bit of water onto the tarpaulin, just enough to get it nice and wet. Then let the slipping and sliding begin! It's super fun and thanks to the washing-up liquid, you'll get clean, too!

HELPFUL HINTS
- To keep the tarpaulin slippery, add a little bit more washing-up liquid and water from time to time.
- A gentle spray nozzle works best, as a strong water jet might remove too much soap.

Caterpillar Snacks

For a fun outdoor snack, try these simple caterpillars.

STEP 1
Poke a wooden skewer through a bunch of green grapes (however many will fit).

STEP 2
Add two dots of white icing to the end grape and stick on chocolate chips for eyes.

STEP 3
Let this little creature crawl right into your tummy!

Watermelon 'Biscuits'

Here's another outdoor snack that is a little messy, but fun and delicious!

STEP 1
Get a grown-up to cut a watermelon into 2.5 centimetre slices.

STEP 2
Put a slice on a chopping board, then press biscuit cutters through the watermelon to remove edible chunks in fun shapes.

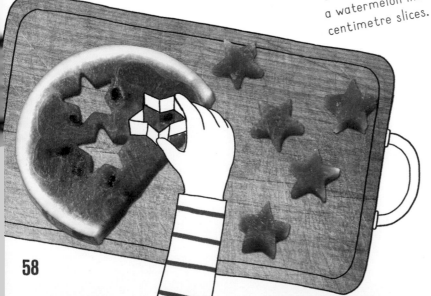

Eat and enjoy!

Make S'mores

This American outdoor snack is fun to make and scrummy to eat.

STEP 1
Put a marshmallow onto a roasting stick. Toast the marshmallow over your campfire until it is warm and soft.

BE SAFE!
Always have an adult supervise activities involving heat or fire.

STEP 2
Put the chocolate bar on one of the biscuits.

STEP 3
Place the marshmallow (still on the stick) on the chocolate. Put the other biscuit on top of the marshmallow. Squeeze the biscuits to hold everything together, then pull out the roasting stick.

STEP 4
Eat and enjoy! Anyone want s'more?

59

Parachute Pals

Send your toys into the sky and watch them sail to the ground with simple parachutes that you can make in minutes.

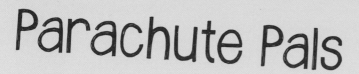

STEP 1
Smooth out the plastic bag on a flat surface. Tie one string to each handle.

STEP 2
Tie the strings to your small toy (it works best if the toy has two arms).

STEP 3
Crumple up the bag and toy in your hands and throw them up into the air. Watch as the bag opens and becomes a parachute for your toy!

HINT
If the toy falls too quickly, remove it and add a slightly lighter one.

FUN IDEA
Using a handheld fan, or one that can be adjusted to point upwards, try keeping your parachute pal in an upward-blowing stream of air.

Soft Toy Zip Wire

Your soft toys will be jealous of the parachutists, so make a zip wire and send them on the ride of their lives!

STEP 1

Tie one end of the string to a tree or another stable object. Stretch the string across a distance of at least 4.5 metres and tie it to another stable object, making sure it is as tight as possible. Also make sure one end of the string is considerably higher than the other.

STEP 2

Tightly wrap a rubber band around your toy and attach a paper clip to the band. Holding the paper clip, lift your toy to test if the rubber band is tight enough and the toy balances correctly. If not, adjust until it does.

STEP 3

Using the paper clip as a hook, attach the toy to the high end of the zip wire. Release it and watch it go!

Water Pistol Painting

This messy art project is the perfect outdoor activity.

STEP 1
Tie a long piece of string between two trees or other sturdy objects. Make it fairly tight.

STEP 2
Use bulldog clips to attach sheets of paper (as many as you like) to the string.

STEP 3
Fill the water pistols with water. Add a few drops of food colouring to each so that you have a different colour in each pistol.

STEP 4
Now pick up the pistols and start squirting! What patterns can you make on the paper? Get creative!

Rainbow Bubble Clouds

Why blow normal bubbles when you could create a rainbow bubble cloud instead? Here's how to do it.

STEP 1
Cut the bottom off the water bottle.

WHAT YOU'LL NEED
- one 500 ml empty water bottle
- scissors
- sock
- rubber band
- food colouring (several colours)
- bubble solution
- shallow dish

STEP 2
Slide the sock over the water bottle and use a rubber band to hold it in place.

STEP 3
Drip food colouring onto the sock in any patterns and colours you like.

STEP 4
Pour some bubble solution into a shallow dish. Dip the sock into the solution, then blow through the neck of the bottle. A rainbow-coloured cloud of bubbles will emerge from the sock!

Pavement Pictures

WHAT YOU`LL NEED
- pavement chalk
- a friend
- a camera

Stuck at home, but wish you were somewhere else? All you need is a camera and some chalk to make your wish come true!

STEP 1

Lie on your path or another good chalk-drawing surface. Strike a pose! Ask a friend to quickly outline your body with the chalk.

STEP 2

Stand up and get to work! Using chalk, draw a scene around your outline. It could be a city, a forest, the sea, space, or anything else you like.

STEP 3

When your artwork is complete, lie back down in the outline. Get your friend to take a picture, then admire the results.

HELPFUL HINT

For best results, take your time and make your chalk colours thick and smooth. The art will show up better in your photos.

Giant String Art

Geometric string art is easy to make and incredibly cool.

WHAT YOU'LL NEED
- about 20 stakes
- lots of brightly-coloured wool or string

STEP 1

Poke the stakes in the ground to make a large circle. Space the stakes as evenly as possible.

WARNING
Stakes can be sharp, so ask an adult for help.

STEP 2

Tie the wool or string to one of the stakes.

HELPFUL HINT

'Stakes' can be almost anything you have handy: sticks, pencils, barbeque skewers, craft sticks, etc. It doesn't really matter how many you use. Twenty is a good starting point, but use more if you like!

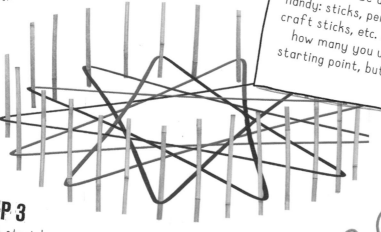

STEP 3

Start stretching the wool or string from one stake to another in a pattern. The pattern can be anything you like, just keep it consistent. Examples would be 'skip four stakes', 'skip seven stakes' and so on. You'll see a cool geometric pattern forming before your eyes!

FUN IDEA

After a satisfying pattern forms, tie off the wool or string. Start a new colour and choose a different pattern. What effects will you create? Try it and see!

Leaf Jumping

This is a classic activity to do in the autumn.

Rake leaves into big piles in your garden, then see what you can do with them! Burrow through the piles, jump into them, jump out of them, try to swim through them, or lie on your back and make 'leaf angels'. The possibilities are endless!

Super Sports Day

Pick some fun events, then invite your friends and family to a super sports day!

You could try running races, sack races, egg-and-spoon relays, skipping races, three-legged races, or anything else you like. You could even invent silly sports such as potato shot-put or fancy dress hula hooping. Give prizes to the winners of each event or the winning team. The aim is to get moving and have fun!

Leaf Rubbings

After you've finished jumping around, choose a few interesting leaves and use them to make some cool nature artwork.

WHAT YOU`LL NEED
- leaves
- thin white paper
- crayons

STEP 1

Find an unusual leaf and place it on a flat surface. Cover the leaf with a sheet of white paper.

STEP 2

Gently rub a crayon back and forth over the leaf. The leaf's edges, veins and texture will make the crayon marks appear darker in some places than others. An image of the leaf will begin to form!

FUN IDEAS
- Choose different crayon colours for different leaves.
- Use many different crayon colours on the same leaf for a rainbow effect.
- Mount your finished artwork on sheets of black paper. Hang them in your room to create a nature gallery!

Target Tower

Set 'em up and knock 'em down! Test your target-shooting skills using just a few household things.

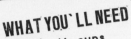

WHAT YOU`LL NEED
- 10 plastic cups
- cotton buds
- straws

STEP 1
Stack the plastic cups in a pyramid-shaped tower.

Disc Golf

Disc golf is a real sport with lots of rules, but you can play a simpler version anywhere. Here's how to do it.

WHAT YOU`LL NEED
- two or more players
- one flying disc per player
- paper and pencil to keep score

STEP 1
Together, all players look around and identify a distant object that will be the target, or 'hole'.

STEP 2

Insert a cotton bud into a straw.

STEP 3

Lying about 2 metres from the tower, put the other end of the straw into your mouth. Puff hard to blast the cotton bud out of the straw. Try to knock over all 10 cups. How many goes will it take?

WARNING
Never suck a straw when it has a cotton bud in it.

STEP 2

Players take turns throwing their discs towards the 'hole'. After everyone has thrown once, they go to their disc, pick it up and take another throw. The goal is to hit the 'hole' with the fewest possible throws.

STEP 3

When everyone has hit the 'hole', write down each player's number of throws.

STEP 4

Everyone identifies the next 'hole' and the whole process starts again.

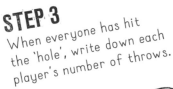

HELPFUL HINT
The person with the lowest score wins the disc golf tournament!

Laser Beam Maze

Would you make a good spy? Find out by navigating this tricky 'laser beam' maze. You'll have to be extra nimble to succeed!

STEP 1

Wrap red string or wool in a crazy zigzag pattern between a selection of trees, poles, chairs, or any other objects in your garden. The pattern should be loose enough for people's bodies to fit through, but tight enough to make it challenging.

STEP 2

Try to climb through the 'laser beams' without touching any of them. Can you do it? Let all your friends take turns, too.

TIP

Ask an adult to help you set up the maze to make sure that it's safe.

Giant Crosswords

Follow these instructions to make an outdoor version of a classic indoor game. Wait for a day that isn't windy, though, or else your 'tiles' will blow away!

WHAT YOU'LL NEED
- 102 sheets of A4 paper
- marker pen

STEP 1

Write one big letter on each sheet of paper to make the 'tiles'. Refer to the table to see how many of each letter you need.

STEP 2

Put the tiles into a big bag. Let each player reach into the bag and pick seven tiles.

STEP 4

After each turn, a player reaches into the bag and picks enough tiles to replace the ones just played. Players always start each turn with seven tiles.

STEP 3

Players take turns using their tiles to lay out words on the ground. They can build on each other's words, crossword-style.

NUMBER OF TILES NEEDED

A x 9	H x 2	O x 8	V x 2
B x 2	I x 9	P x 2	W x 4
C x 2	J x 1	Q x 1	X x 1
D x 4	K x 1	R x 6	Y x 2
E x 12	L x 4	S x 4	Z x 1
F x 2	M x 2	T x 6	
G x 3	N x 6	U x 4	

Blank x 2 (can be any letter of the player's choosing)

THE WINNER

After all of the tiles have been picked from the bag, the first player to get rid of their tiles wins the game!

BEAT Boredom on the MOVE

Bored on a long journey? Put down your phone and try out these 27 ideas for having fun whilst travelling.

Whether around town or on holiday, in a car, train, or plane, there are loads of ways to keep yourself occupied. You don't need to prepare or take a lot with you to have fun.

Ask your friends and family to join in and enjoy the ride together!

Snack Pack

Junk food is convenient and easy to find on a long journey, but with just a little time and thought, you can put together a snack pack full of better tasting, more nutritious food to take with you. Pick some snacks and pack them up!

PROTEIN

Bring some protein to help you feel full on your journey. Try these:
- nuts
- yogurt tubes
- cheese cubes or sticks
- slices of cooked meat such as turkey, chicken or salami

FRUIT

Hard fruit that doesn't squash easily is great for travelling. How about:
- small apples
- dried fruit

VEGGIES

Chop up some colourful vegetables and bring small containers of houmous or guacamole for dipping:
- baby carrots
- celery sticks
- sliced pepper
- sugar snap peas

DRINKS

You need to stay hydrated when you travel. Pack plenty of drinks, including:
- water
- low-sugar juice

CARBS

When choosing carbs, try and stick to the healthier stuff, such as:
- granola
- pretzels
- popcorn

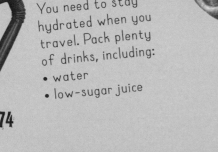

Mystery Grab Bags

Long rides feel easier if they are divided into short segments and mystery grab bags are one way to break things up. You'll need to prepare this activity before your journey begins, so get started now!

STEP 1
Together with all participants, look at a map of your journey. Identify about ten milestones along the way (towns, roads, landmarks, etc.).

STEP 2
Each participant finds one small surprise per milestone and puts it in a bag. The surprises can be anything — small toys, sweets, photos and so on.

STEP 3
During the trip, when a milestone is reached, all players get to reach into someone else's bag and pull out a surprise. What will it be? You never know, but the curiosity is part of the fun!

'I Spy' Bottle

An 'I Spy' bottle requires a little pre-travel prep, but it's worth it. It will keep you entertained for hours!

WHAT YOU`LL NEED
- empty, dry, clear water bottle with the label removed
- 20 to 30 small objects, such as coins, buttons, shells, paper clips, beads, or anything that will fit into the bottle
- rice

STEP 1
Put the small objects into the water bottle.

STEP 2
Fill the bottle most of the way with rice, leaving about 2.5 cm space at the top. Screw the top on tightly.

STEP 3
Shake and roll the bottle to mix the rice and the objects. This will take a while, so be patient.

TWO WAYS TO PLAY
1. Make a list of everything you put into the bottle. Shake and roll the bottle until you find every object. How long will it take?
2. Try to find as many objects as possible in a set amount of time.

Compete to discover the 'I Spy' master!

Very Interesting!

You'll see many interesting things when you're on the move. Use these things as conversation starters to make the time fly by!

THE RULES

1. All players take turns pointing out something they think is interesting. It could be anything — a really big tree, an animal, a landmark, a cloud...

2. When a person points something out, they must explain why they chose it and why they think it's interesting.

3. All the other players get to make one comment about the item. If they also find the item interesting, they could say why. They could also explain if they don't like the item, if it reminds them of something else, or just anything that comes to mind.

WOW!

FUN IDEA

Make a list of all the things identified in this game. It will be a great keepsake to remind you of your journey!

Travel Scrapbook

Making a travel scrapbook is a fun way to capture your on-the-move adventures. You'll be able to look back at your journeys, remember them forever and share them with your friends and family.

WHAT YOU`LL NEED
- a noteboook with blank pages
- sticky tape or glue stick
- coloured markers, pens and pencils

STEP 1
Collect small, flat keepsakes throughout the first day of your journey. Look at the list on this page for ideas.

STEP 2
In the evening, tape or glue your mementos in the first pages of your journal. Put the date at the top of the page and write down the highlights of your day.

STEP 3
Use markers, pens and pencils to decorate the pages and add any other drawings of things you've seen.

STEP 4
Repeat steps 1–3 every day. When your trip ends, you'll have a permanent record of everything you saw and did!

THINGS TO COLLECT
- tickets
- brochures
- stamps
- photos
- maps
- leaves
- flowers

Stories by the Sentence

Writing a whole story can be tricky, but it's simple when you do it sentence by sentence!

The next person adds a sentence, then the next person adds one and so on.

Your story can be short and sweet, or it might be a whole novel if you're on a really long journey and you just keep going...

Begin by saying just one sentence to start your story – the weirder, the better.

Silly Scribbles

After creating a story together, why not try creating a piece of artwork, too? This game works best if you play in pairs.

Each player starts with a blank sheet of paper and draws a scribble or a simple shape. Both players swap their sheets of paper and then try to make their partner's scribble into a drawing or a picture. The sillier, the better!

Repeat to make a collection of scribbles, or for some speedy scribble fun, try setting yourselves a time limit to complete each drawing.

Napkin Roses

Do you ever feel like the wait for your food in a restaurant can take forevvvveeeeeerrrrrr? If you do, try making some napkin roses to pass the time.

STEP 1
Completely unfold a paper napkin, then roll it into a loose tube.

STEP 2
Starting about 3 centimetres from the top of the tube, twist until you reach roughly the halfway point of the tube.

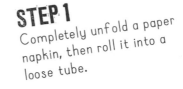

STEP 3
Pull up the bottom corner to make a leaf. Twist the rest of the tube to finish the stem.

STEP 4
Gently bend the loose part of the tube until the petals look pretty. Then give the rose to someone you love!

Straw Wrapper Snakes

When you've finished making roses, switch to straw wrapper snakes instead. These little creatures will keep your hands busy and your mind off your empty tummy.

STEP 1
Flatten two paper straw wrappers and lay them on a table with their ends meeting at a right angle.

STEP 2
Fold the bottom wrapper over along the edge of the top wrapper.

STEP 3
Now the first wrapper has become the bottom wrapper. Fold it over the top wrapper like you did in step 2.

STEP 4
Repeat, alternating wrappers, to make a long accordion-fold snake. Add a face and a forked tongue if you like. See how many you can make before your food arrives!

On-the-Go Exercises

Long days in a car, plane or train can leave you feeling stiff and sore from lack of movement. Try these on-the-go exercises to help you loosen up and relax.

THE TUMMY TESTER

Sit up straight and breathe in. Then breathe out through your nose whilst sucking your tummy muscles up and in, like you're trying to touch your spine with your navel. Hold for 10 to 20 seconds.

BICEP CURLS

Hold a small but weighty object, such as a full plastic bottle, in one hand with your palm facing up. Keeping the upper arm still, curl your forearm up, then slowly lower it. Repeat 12 times with each arm.

SEATED MARCH

Keeping one foot on the floor, raise the other leg as high as you can. Lower that leg, then raise the other one. Alternate your legs to march in place for 30 to 50 repetitions (reps).

CALF & TOE RAISES

For calf raises, keep your toes on the floor and gently lift your heels as high as you can. For toe raises, keep the heels on the floor and slowly raise the toes. Try 30 reps of each, or alternate between calf and toe raises for a 60-second workout.

Dream Interpretation

Share your wackiest dreams with your travel buddies, then ask them to take turns explaining what they think they mean.

So you were on the Moon drinking tea with a camel? That must mean that you'll become a zookeeper. Or maybe you were just thirsty at the time... See who can come up with the silliest explanations!

Two Truths and a Lie

How well do you know the other travellers? You're about to find out!

Each person tells two truths and one lie about themselves. Your job is to decide which is which. The person who is correct the most wins the game!

truth!

lie!

TIP

The game works best if your truths are a little unusual or wacky. They will blend in better with your lie and make it sound less obvious.

Travel Bingo

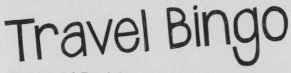

BINGO! Find five items in a row to win this fun game.

STEP 1
Each player draws a five-by-five grid on a sheet of paper. Label the middle square FREE.

STEP 2
Each player fills in the remaining spots on the grid with 24 travel-related items. You can make up your own items, or use the list on this page.

dog in car	postbox	bridge	graveyard	wild animal
coach	cow	petrol station	ambulance	helicopter
caravan		FREE	motorbike	train
aeroplane	speed limit sign		horse	limousine
rain		horse	cyclist	taxi

STEP 3
Players cross off each item as they see it. The first person to cross off a full row, column, or diagonal line yells 'BINGO!' and wins the game.

Be the DJ

Let's face it, behind every good journey lies a GREAT soundtrack!

To get your toes tapping and your fingers snapping, connect your phone to your car's sound system. Take requests from the other passengers, then crank it up and sing along. Just remember to be fair and give everyone a turn. Yes, your music is great, but everyone has their favourite tracks. Play them all!

Guess the Song

This game could be very easy or very hard, depending on the musical talent of the players!

The first player picks a popular song or tune and shares it with the other players by humming it — no words allowed! The other travellers then race to guess the song. The person who guesses correctly gets to choose and hum the next tune.

Would You Rather?

Some questions are impossible to answer... but it can be fun to try! A game of 'Would You Rather?' gets everyone thinking and talking.

STEP 1
Everyone comes up with a few questions and writes each question on a separate slip of paper. You could use the questions on this page or make up your own.

STEP 2
Players should fold up their slips of paper and put them into a cup or a small bag.

STEP 3
Take turns reaching into the cup and pulling out a slip of paper. Each player has to answer the question they've picked and give their reasons. Everyone else should feel free to join in with their own answers, if they like. You never know what you might learn about your fellow travellers!

WOULD YOU RATHER...
- Have the power to be invisible or to fly?
- Travel 100 years into the future or the past?
- Have true love or a billion dollars?
- Eat a dead insect or a live worm?

- Be bald or hairy all over?
- Spend the rest of your life indoors or outdoors?
- Live without electricity or running water?

20 Questions

In this classic game, you get 20 questions to guess a secret. You need to think fast and make those questions count!

Are you an astronaut?

THE RULES

1. One player thinks of a person, place or thing. He or she says which it is.

2. The other players take turns asking questions about the secret answer. The questions must be formed to give only 'Yes' or 'No' answers. For example, if the secret thing is a person, a player might ask, 'Is this person male?' But they could not ask, 'Is this person male or female?'

3. If someone guesses the secret before 20 questions have been asked, they win and get to choose the secret for the next round. If no one can guess the answer within 20 questions, the current secret holder wins and gets to choose again.

HELPFUL HINT

Ask broad questions first. Narrow things down as you eliminate big chunks of information. Logical thinking really helps in this game!

Postcard Journal

Writing and sending postcards is a great way to share your adventures, but why not try collecting postcards for yourself so that you can look back and remember your trip when you get home?

WHAT YOU'LL NEED
- postcards (one per day)
- pen or pencil

STEP 1
Every day on your trip, buy a postcard showing something you did or saw that day.

STEP 2
On the back of the postcard, write yourself a short note explaining the highlights of your day. Tuck the postcard away in your travel bag.

STEP 3
When you get home, hole punch the postcards. Use a ribbon to tie them together into a booklet. Look through your postcard journal whenever you want to relive your adventure.

FUN IDEA
You can stamp and post your postcards to yourself. When you get home, they'll be waiting for you and they'll look all cool and official with their stamps.

Pipe Cleaner Art

A packet of multicoloured pipe cleaners (available at any pound shop) provides hours of on-the-go entertainment.

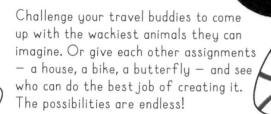

Challenge your travel buddies to come up with the wackiest animals they can imagine. Or give each other assignments — a house, a bike, a butterfly — and see who can do the best job of creating it. The possibilities are endless!

Puzzles and Patterns

Whilst you're shopping for those pipe cleaners, pick up some puzzle books. Pound shops sell books full of word searches, Sudoku puzzles, crosswords, brain-teasers and even intricate colouring patterns.

It's a travel bonanza. Grab a few books and why not treat yourself to a special pen or some new coloured pencils whilst you're at it? You'll be ready to entertain yourself for hours!

Where in the World?

This travel game doesn't require any special equipment or memory skills, but some geography knowledge — and a little quick thinking — will be a big help.

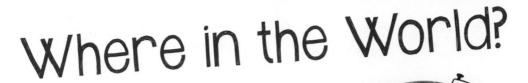

STEP 1
One player names a geographic location. It could be a country, a city, a monument, a body of water and so on.

STEP 2
The next player must name a new geographic location that begins with the last letter of the previous location.

STEP 3
The game continues with each player naming a new location. If a player can't name a location, he or she is OUT!

THE WINNER
The last person left in the game is the winner. Well done! You certainly know your way around the world!

Find the Alphabet

This game can take some time, but who cares? You've got nothing but time when you're on a long car or train journey. This game will make the miles disappear!

STEP 1

Each player writes down all the letters of the alphabet on their paper.

STEP 2

Look out of the windows. Try to spot each letter of the alphabet IN ORDER (first A, then B and so on). Cross each letter off your list as you spot it. The first person to find all 26 letters wins the game!

SPEEDY VERSION

For a shorter game, find and cross off the letters in any order, or work as a team. See how quickly you can find the entire alphabet!

HELPFUL HINT

Letters can be anywhere — on signs, number plates, buildings, car bumper stickers and so on. Anything goes!

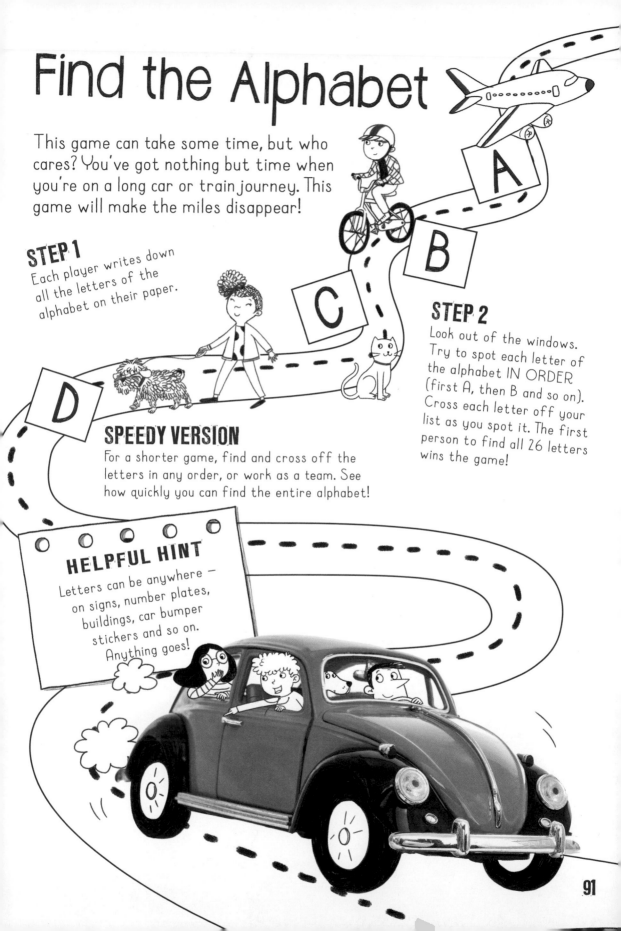

Number Plate Checklist

If you need something to keep you entertained during a long car journey, use the other cars around you to play a game.

Ideas

- Before your trip, print out a list of vehicle country codes for number plates. Try to spot and check off a number plate from as many countries as you can during your travels. See who can find the most countries!
- Number plates contain a mixture of letters and numbers. Some include short words like HAT or CAN. Keep an eye out and see how many words you can find!
- Try to find a number plate that starts with each letter of the alphabet.

Spot It!

Cars, cars, cars! If you're travelling by car, look out of the window and try to spot the following types.

Volkswagen Beetle "IT'S HERBIE!"

Car with one headlight out "FIDDLE!"

Removal van "LET'S GO!"

Dented car "DING DING!"

Yellow car "BANANA!"

When you do, be the first to shout the correct phrase for each car and earn one point. The first player to get 20 points wins!

Memory Master

Who has the best memory? Play this classic travel game to find out! You don't need any supplies, just your imagination and at least two players. It'll keep you busy for hours!

STEP 1

Player 1 says, 'I went on a road trip and I brought...' and then names something starting with the letter A. Let's say the player decides to bring an APPLE.

STEP 2

Player 2 says, 'I went on a road trip and I brought an APPLE and a...' and then names something starting with the letter B.

STEP 3

The game continues with each player repeating all the items named previously, then adding an item that starts with the next letter in the alphabet. If a player forgets an item, he or she is OUT and the game continues without them.

THE WINNER

The last person left in the game is the Memory Master. Well done!

Road Trip Scavenger Hunt

What will you see on your journey? Take your best guess before you leave, then compete in a fun road trip scavenger hunt! Here's how:

STEP 1
Together with your travel buddies, create a list of ten to twenty things you might see on your trip. The example list on this page is for a trip to the beach. Your list might be different, depending on your destination.

STEP 2
Write or print out one copy of the list for each person.

STEP 3
Everyone looks for the items on the list throughout the trip. Check off each item as you see it. Who will finish their list first?

- ☐ SANDCASTLE
- ☐ SURFER
- ☐ SHELL
- ☐ SEAWEED
- ☐ BEACH TOWEL
- ☐ DOG PLAYING IN SEA
- ☐ LIFEGUARD
- ☐ ICE CREAM
- ☐ SUN CREAM
- ☐ SUNBURNT PERSON
- ☐ SEAGULL
- ☐ BOAT
- ☐ DRIFTWOOD
- ☐ PIER

Virtual Hide-and-Seek

Hide-and-seek is a great game to play at home, but you can bring it with you on your travels if you use your imagination!

TIPS

- It works best if you all 'hide' in the same home, or are familiar with each player's home.
- You must be able to fit in your imaginary hiding place, so no hiding inside a toaster or a tissue box!
- You can hide in plain sight. If you want to be sitting at the kitchen table, that's just fine.
- There is no limit on the number of questions. The game continues until you are 'found'!